ACTIVATING ANGELIC RE-ENFORCEMENT

"Are they not all ministering spirits, sent forth to minister for them who shall be heirs of salvation?"

Hebrews 1:14

by

Franklin N. Abazie

Activating Angelic Re-enforcement
COPYRIGHT 2017 BY Franklin N Abazie
ISBN: 978-0-9966-263-0-9

All right reserved. This book or any portion thereof may not be reproduced or used in any manner whatsoever without the express written permission of the publisher, except for the use of brief quotations in a book review. All Bible quotes are from King James Version and others as noted.

Published by: F N ABAZIE PUBLISHING HOUSE- aka, Empowerment Bookstore.

That I may publish with the voice of thanksgiving and tell of all thy wondrous works.
Psalms 26:7

To order additional copies, wholesales
or booking:
Call the Church office (973-372-7518),
or Empowerment Bookstore Hotline (973-393-8518)

Worship address:
343 Sanford Avenue Newark New Jersey 07106
Administrative Head Office address:
33 Schley Street Newark New Jersey 07112
Email:pastorfranknto@yahoo.com
Website www.fnabaziehealingministries.org
Publishing House: www.fnabaziepublishinghouse.org

This book is a production of F N Abazie Publishing House.
A publication Arms of Miracle of God Ministries 2017.
Second Edition

CONTENTS

THE MANDATE OF THE COMMISSION iv
ARMS OF THE COMMISSION v
INTRODUCTION vi
CHAPTER 1
1 Who Are Angels? 1
CHAPTER 2
2 The Function of Angels 6
CHAPTER 3
3 Prayer of Salvation 26
CHAPTER 4
4 About The Author 35

THE MANDATE OF THE COMMISSION

"THE MOMENT IS DUE TO IMPACT YOUR WORLD THROUGH THE REVIVAL OF THE HEALING & MIRACLE MINISTRY OF JESUS CHRIST OF NAZARETH."

"I AM SENDING YOU TO RESTORE HEALTH UNTO THEE AND I WILL HEAL THEE OF THY WOUNDS, SAID THE LORD OF HOST."

ARMS OF THE COMMISSION

1) F N Abazie Ministries-Miracle of God Ministries (Miracle Chapel Intl)

2) F N Abazie TV Ministries: Global Television Ministry Outreach

3) F N Abazie Radio Ministries: Radio Broadcasting Outreach

4) F N Abazie Publishing House: Book Publication

5) F N Abazie Bible School: also called Word of Healing Bible School (W.O.H.B.S)

6) F N Abazie Evangelistic Ass: Miracle of God Ministries: Global Crusade

7) Empowerment Bookstore: Book distribution

8) F N Abazie Helping Hands: Meeting the help of the needy world wide

9) F N Abazie Disaster Recovery Mission: Global Disaster Recovery

10) F N Abazie Prison Ministry: Prison Ministry for all convicts "Second chance"

Some of our ministry arms are waiting the appointed time to commence.

INTRODUCTION

This publication is a book, designed to re-enforce our guardian angels on duty. One must recognize that God sent forth His Angels to assist and help us in the time of need. It is written, *"Behold, I send an Angel before thee, to keep thee in the way, and to bring thee into the place which I have prepared."* Exodus 23:20

The *Angels* of the Lord are *ministering spirits*. In my opinion, Angels are sent *forth to ministering protection, deliverance, and breakthrough* to us. Quite often, some of us offend the angel of God and think there is *"nothing wrong with that."* It is written, *"Beware of him, and obey his voice, provoke him not; for he will not pardon your transgressions: for my name is in him. But if thou shalt indeed obey his voice, and do all that I speak; then I will be an enemy unto thine enemies, and an adversary unto thine adversaries."* Exodus 23:21-22

Only a fool will think that he/she does not need the help of an angel. For the most part unless *we obey the voice of the angels of God* assigned over our lives, we will forever struggle with a lot of things in life. This book *"Activating Angelic Re-enforcement"* is a book, designed put our angels on duty. As long as you apply the relevant technique explained in this publication, your guardian angel will resume His duties over your life.

Who are Angels?

In one sentence, Angels are *"ministering Spirits."* Angels minister to us the same way they ministered to Jesus. It is written "… and the angels ministered unto him." (Mark 1:13) We were told, *"Are they not all ministering spirits, sent forth to minister for them who shall be heirs of salvation?"* (Hebrews 1:14)

I, therefore, encourage you to overlook the mechanics of my grammar but pay attention to what the Holy Spirit is saying concerning our guardian angels. "What is man, that thou art mindful of him? and the son of man, that thou visitest him? For thou hast made him a little lower than the angels, and hast crowned him with glory and honor. (Psalms 8:4-5) In my own opinion, this small book will help you activate your guardian angels.

Happy reading

HOW TO ENCOUNTER THE HOLY GHOST

One will think just about anybody can encounter they Holy Spirit. Often, what you call the Holy Spirit is not the voice of the Holy Spirit. So many of us *hear our own self, our desire and we think we* heard from the Lord. If you do not know Him, how can you hear Him?

We were told, *"And a stranger will they not follow, but will flee from him: for they know not the voice of strangers."* (John 10:5) For unless you repent of your sins, God will not restore your life. For unless you repent of your sins, you will miss your heavenly encounter with the Holy Ghost

You must repent your sins and be born again.

1) Acknowledge that you are a sinner and that He died for you. (Romans 3:23)

2) Repent of your sins. (Acts 3:19, Luke 13:5, 2 Peter 3:9)

3) Believe in your heart that Jesus died for your sin. (Romans 10:10)

4) Confess Jesus as the Lord over your life. (Romans 10:10, Acts 2:21)

Now repeat this Prayer after me

Say Lord Jesus, I accept you today, as my Lord and my savior, forgive me of my sins wash me with your blood. Right now, I believe, I am sanctified, I am save, I am free, I am free from the Power of sin to serve the Lord Jesus. Thank you Lord for saving me. Amen.

---HE IS OUR CREATOR---

1) We must worship Him, because He is our creator.

2) We must worship Him, because He is sovereign.

3) We must worship Him, because we are made in His image.

4) We must worship Him, because our worship attracts His presence.

5) We must worship Him, for our faith in Him to grow.

6) We must worship Him, to nourish and reactivate our spirit man.

7) We must worship Him, because it activates our faith in Him.

8) We must worship Him, to retain the Joy of the Lord.

9) We worship Him to evict depression, envy, and malice.

10) We worship Him to be happy and to escape strive and hatred.

11) We worship Him to escape bitterness, stress, anger, and misery.

BENEFITS OF OUR WORSHIP

1) Worship is medicinal, it heals our soul, body and spirit man.

2) Worship is supernatural, it position us for constant victory in life.

3) Worship is spiritual, it grants us hope and faith in Him.

4) Worship is a mystery, it keeps us on the winning side of life.

5) Worship is faithful, it gives us encourages us to put us the fight.

6) Worship is strengthening, it reduces the size of our problem.

7) Worship is devotional, it proves our loyalty.

8) Worship is humbling, it proves our meekness before God.

9) Worship is power, it grants us access into signs and wonders.

10) Worship is divine, it accelerates divine intervention.

11) Worship is pleasing, God takes pleasure in it.

12) Worship is a treasure, it catches the attention of God.

13) Worship is rewarding, it brings God into our trials.

14) Worship is reciprocal, it provokes God to act.

15) Worship is glorifying, it magnifies God in our situation.

16) Worship is a blessing, it opens the flood gate of heaven.

17) Worship is our responsibility, it delivers us out of obscurity.

18) Worship is deliverance, it releases us out of captivity.

19) Worship is deeper, God looks for us to prove His divinity.

20) Worship is a reminder, God remembers His promises.

21) Worship is protection, we secure His protection.

22) Worship is unity, it grants us angelic help.

ANGELIC INTERVENTION PRAYER POINT

"And he said, Let me go, for the day breaketh. And he said, I will not let thee go, except thou bless me." Genesis 32:26

Holy Spirit of God frustrate and disappoint, every one that is against my life and family, in the name of Jesus.

Father Lord destroy every demonic networks and traps against my progress in life in the name of Jesus.

Fire of God, destroy every demonic projection and curses against my life and destiny in the name of Jesus.

Every spell and curses pronounced against my destiny, break, in the name of Jesus.

Hand of God cage every power militating against my rising in life, in the name of Jesus.

Power of God silent every voice raising a counter motion against my elevation, in the mighty name of Jesus.

Blood of Jesus neutralize every spirit of Balaam hired to hinder my life, ministry, and career, the name of Jesus.

Fire of God destroy every curse that I have brought into my life through ignorance and disobedience, break by fire, in the name of Jesus.

Ancient of day destroy every power harassing my ministry in the name of Jesus.

Father God deliver me from invincible forces militating against my life and destiny.

Power of God frustrate every coven and demonic network, designed to frustrate and hinder my success in life, in the name of Jesus.

I dismantle every strong hold designed to imprison my talent in the mighty name of Jesus.

I reject every cycle of frustration, in the name of Jesus.

Power of God paralyze every agent assigned to frustrate my life in the name of Jesus.

Finger of God, grant me supernatural speed against all my contenders in the name of Jesus.

By the blood of Jesus, I destroy every familiar spirit caging my life and career.

Fire of God arrest every demonic agents, assigned to police my destiny and marriage.

By the blood of Jesus, I proclaim no weapon fashioned against me shall ever prosper.

Holy Spirit of God break me through and forward in life in the mighty name of Jesus.

God, smash me and renew my strength, in the name of Jesus.

Holy Spirit, open my eyes to see beyond the visible to the invisible, in the name of Jesus.

Father Lord grant me strength and power in the name of Jesus

O Lord, liberate my spirit to follow the leading of the Holy Spirit.

Holy Spirit, teach me to pray through problems instead of praying about, it in the name of Jesus.

Father Lord, deliver me from the false accusation in life, in the name of Jesus.

By the blood of Jesus, every evil spiritual padlock and evil chain hindering my success, be roasted, in the name of Jesus.

By the blood of Jesus I rebuke every spirit of spiritual deafness and blindness in my life, in the name of Jesus.

Father Lord, empower me to dominate the enemy of my destiny in the name of Jesus.

Jesus Christ of Nazareth, heal my infirmities in the name of Jesus

Lord, anoint my eyes and my ears that they may see and hear wondrous things from heaven.

Father Lord, anoint me with power and authority to dominate all my enemies in the name of Jesus.

Fire of God roast every giant rising up against my life and career.

Holy Spirit of God destroy all my oppressors in the name of Jesus.

Angels of good new, bring my good news to me in the mighty name of Jesus.

Every strong man holding me down, lose your hold now in the name of Jesus.

I nullify every demonic prediction over my life in the name of Jesus.

By the blood of Jesus, I flush out every polluted deposit of the enemy in my life.

By the blood of Jesus, I paralyze every enemy of my promotion in the name of Jesus.

Father Lord, destroy any power tormenting my life that is not from you.

Holy Ghost fire, ignite the fire of revival in my life.

By the blood of Jesus, I declare victory over every conflicting trial

By the Blood of Jesus, I command the arrest of every demonic spirit, militating against my life

By the blood of Jesus, I proclaimed the blood of Jesus, over every device of the enemy.

By the blood of Jesus, I revoke stagnation and hardship over my life in the name of Jesus.

Holy Ghost fire, destroy every satanic arrangement in my life, in the name of Jesus.

"Thinkest thou that I cannot now pray to my Father, and he shall presently give me more than twelve legions of angels?"

Matthew 26:53

"For he shall give his angels charge over thee, to keep thee in all thy ways."

Psalms 91:11

HIS DESTINY WAS THE **CROSS....**

HIS PURPOSE WAS **LOVE.....**

HIS REASON WAS **YOU....**

CHAPTER 1

WHO ARE ANGELS?

"Are they not all ministering spirits, sent forth to minister for them who shall be heirs of salvation?"
Hebrews 1:14

Although theologians and scholars have put together some fantastic definitions of Angels. In my own simple opinion, *angels are ministering spirit*, sent forth by *God to minister to all our challenges in life*. There are so many inexplicable things we can recount in life that, one will say this must be the hand of God. It is written, *"This is the Lord's doing; it is marvellous in our eyes."* (Psalms 118:23)

Angels are spiritual beings created by God to minister to our lives. God is still using His angels to do marvelous things in the life of most of us that believe. The New Testament put it this way, "This was the Lord's doing, and it is marvellous in our eyes?" Mark 12:11

The story of the three Hebrew boys in the midst of a fire, remains a mystery to date. It will take only the hand of God to change the life of any man who dares to believe.

It is written, *"Jesus said unto him, If thou canst believe, all things are possible to him that believeth."* Mark 9:23

It is written Then Nebuchadnezzar spake, and said, Blessed be the God of Shadrach, Meshach, and Abednego, who hath sent his angel, and delivered his servants that trusted in him, and have changed the king's word, and yielded their bodies, that they might not serve nor worship any god, except their own God. (Daniel 3:28)

In my own simple understanding, for unless you trust in God, and have faith in God, you will never experience angelic intervention in life.

It is written, *"My God hath sent his angel, and hath shut the lions' mouths, that they have not hurt me: forasmuch as before him innocency was found in me; and also before thee, O king, have I done no hurt."* Daniel 6:22

ANGELS ARE AGENTS OF DIVINE PROVIDENCE

Although angels are divine agents of rescue and deliverance, they are also God's agents of divine providence. It was an angel that ministered to Jesus and sustained him. (See Mark 1:13, Matthew 4:1-11) It was an angel of God that brought food for Elijah at his weakest moment.

It was an angel of God the rescued peter

and Paul both from prison houses. (Acts 12:1-10, Acts 16:25-26) For the most part God's agents watch over our lives. The angels of God are ministering spirits, they minister to our lives, in a dream and visions.

GOD'S ANGELS EXECUTE DIVINE JUDGMENT

Although arc angel Gabriel declared openly of the birth of Jesus Christ, he also declared the birth of Samson and John the Baptist. God's loyal angels are loyal at His command. It is written, "bless the Lord, ye his angels, that excel in strength, that do his commandments, hearkening unto the voice of his word." Psalms 103:20

HINDERANCE TO THE MINISTRY OF ANGELS

~Unbelief

"Suffer not thy mouth to cause thy flesh to sin; neither say thou before the angel, that it was an error: wherefore should God be angry at thy voice, and destroy the work of thine hands?" Ecll 5:6

Unless we believe in the ministry of angels, we will forever miss experiencing angelic encounter in life. Unless you believe in angels, you will never experience the ministry of an angel. It is written, "And he answered, Fear not: for they that be with us are more than they that be with them." Unbelief in the ministry of angels will hinder anyone from experiencing angelic help in life.

Zachariah, the father of John the baptist, became dumb because he doubted the voice of the angel of God. It is written, "And, behold, thou shalt be dumb, and not able to speak, until the day that these things shall be performed, because thou believest not my words, which shall be fulfilled in their season." Luke 1:20

Although unbelief hinders angelic experience, it also hinder and withholds our miracle from the Lord. If you must experience God, then you must believe in the ministry of angels.

~Fear of the unknown

"And he answered, Fear not: for they that be with us are more than they that be with them." 2 King 6:16

Most young believers are scared of the unknown. Unless we transform our believe system we will forever miss our miracle.

~Lack of personal conviction that God is able

It is written, "And Manoah said unto the angel of the Lord, I pray thee, let us detain thee, until we shall have made ready a kid for thee." (Judges 13:15) Unless we are convicted by the ministry of an angel, we will not be able to fulfil our angelic revelation. In my opinion lack of personal conviction in the ministry of angels will hinder anyone from experiencing God in His angelic dimension.

CHAPTER 2
THE FUNCTION OF ANGELS

"Behold, I send an Angel before thee, to keep thee in the way, and to bring thee into the place which I have prepared".
Exodus 23:20

Although there are *five different types of angels*, each angel is assigned to a particular function. It was only *Lucifer* who operated in two unique offices and had the privilege of a double function. Arc *angel Lucifer*, could *proclaim the glory of God* and could also *protect the glory of God.* For the most part, *Lucifer* had a broader function as an angel, this resulted into jealousy and rebellion against the Almighty God.

It is written, "How art thou fallen from heaven, O Lucifer, son of the morning! How art thou cut down to the ground, which didst weaken the nations! For thou hast said in thine heart, I will ascend into heaven, I will exalt my throne above the stars of God: I will sit also upon the mount of the congregation, in the sides of the north: I will ascend above the heights of the clouds; I will be like the most High. Yet thou shalt be brought down to hell, to the sides of the pit. They that see thee shall narrowly look upon thee, and consider thee, saying, Is this the man that made the earth to tremble, that did shake kingdoms; That made the world as a wilderness, and destroyed the cities thereof; that opened not the house of his prisoners?" Isaiah 14:12-17

Although Cherubim angels protect the glory of the Lord, it is seraphim angels that declare the glory of the Lord. Lucifer was a special angel, who had the ability to operate from both office.

Lucifer was even more powerful because he was an arc angel. Arc angels also mean chief angels. They were in charge and commanded other angels. Among other arc angels were arc angels Michael and Gabriel. Arc angel Gabriel is the chief messenger angel, while arc angel Michael is the chief defender angel.

It was arc angel Michael who initiated the fight against the rebellious angel Lucifer. *"And there was war in heaven: Michael and his angels fought against the dragon; and the dragon fought and his angels."* Rev 12:7

Angel Lucifer lost the fight and he was cast down into the earth. *"Yet thou shalt be brought down to hell, to the sides of the pit."* Isaiah 14:15

It is written, "And the great dragon was cast out, that old serpent, called the Devil, and Satan, which deceiveth the whole world: he was cast out into the earth, and his angels were cast out with him." Rev 12:9

It is written...

"Thou hast been in Eden the garden of God; every precious stone was thy covering, the sardius, topaz, and the diamond, the beryl, the onyx, and the jasper, the sapphire, the emerald, and the carbuncle, and gold: the workmanship of thy tabrets and of thy pipes was prepared in thee in the day that thou wast created.

Thou art the anointed cherub that covereth; and I have set thee so: thou wast upon the holy mountain of God; thou hast walked up and down in the midst of the stones of fire. Thou wast perfect in thy ways from the day that thou wast created, till iniquity was found in thee.

By the multitude of thy merchandise they have filled the midst of thee with violence, and thou hast sinned: therefore I will cast thee as profane out of the mountain of God: and I will destroy thee, O covering cherub, from the midst of the stones of fire.

Thine heart was lifted up because of thy beauty, thou hast corrupted thy wisdom by reason of thy brightness: I will cast thee to the ground, I will lay thee before kings, that they may behold thee.

Thou hast defiled thy sanctuaries by the multitude of thine iniquities, by the iniquity of thy traffick; therefore will I bring forth a fire from the midst of thee, it shall devour thee, and I will bring thee to ashes upon the earth in the sight of all them that behold thee. All they that know thee among the people shall be astonished at thee: thou shalt be a terror, and never shalt thou be any more." Ezekiel 28:13-19

For the most part *Arc angel Gabriel* was the *messenger angel*. Arc Angel Gabriel also was the messenger angel who announced to Mary about the Holy Child Jesus. (see Luke 1:28-35) It was also *arc angel Gabriel* who also instructed Manoah and His wife, on the birth of Samson.

Angels are not to be worshipped. Although humans were created a little lower than angels, we are not to worship angels. All angels were created pure, without sin, and in a state of perfect holiness. Nevertheless, angels have limitations compares to man, especially in future relationships. Angels are not created in the image of God.

DUTIES OF AN ANGEL

~Agents of God's instruction

Although the angels of God are agents of warning, they are for the most part messengers of a blessing. It was an angel of God that appeared to Manoah's wife to reveal and instruct her about the birth of Samson.

It is written, "And the angel of the Lord appeared unto the woman, and said unto her, Behold now, thou art barren, and bearest not: but thou shalt conceive, and bear a son. Now therefore beware, I pray thee, and drink not wine nor strong drink, and eat not any unclean thing: For, lo, thou shalt conceive, and bear a son; and no razor shall come on his head: for the child shall be a Nazarite unto God from the womb: and he shall begin to deliver Israel out of the hand of the Philistines. Then the woman came and told her husband, saying, A man of God came unto me, and his countenance was like the countenance of an angel of God, very terrible: but I asked him not whence he was, neither told he me his name: But he said unto me, Behold, thou shalt conceive, and bear a son; and now drink no wine nor strong drink, neither eat any unclean thing: for the child shall be a Nazarite to God from the womb to the day of his death." Judges 13:3-7

~Agents of God's direction

It was an angel of God that instructed Joseph on what to do in a dream. It is written "But while he thought on these things, behold, the angel of the Lord appeared unto him in a dream, saying, Joseph, thou son of David, fear not to take unto thee Mary thy wife: for that which is conceived in her is of the Holy Ghost. And she shall bring forth a son, and thou shalt call his name Jesus: for he shall save his people from their sins." Matthew 1:20-21

Again, it was an angel of God that instructed Joseph to escape from the death trap of King Herod.

"But when Herod was dead, behold, an angel of the Lord appeareth in a dream to Joseph in Egypt, Saying, Arise, and take the young child and his mother, and go into the land of Israel: for they are dead which sought the young child's life." Matthew 2:19-20

~The Angels of God are agents of protection

It is written "For he shall give his angels charge over thee, to keep thee in all thy ways." (Psalms 91:11) David said I laid me down and slept; I awaked; for the Lord sustained me.

Unless God's angels protect us against the wiles and schemes of the devil, we will remain vulnerable to the devil. God's angels are agents of protection, against any impending danger in life. God's angels are agents of protection according to psalms ninety one verse eleven and Daniel chapter six verse twenty two.

~The Angels of God are agents of persecution

The angels of God, do not only protect & deliver us from the forces of evil, they also fight for us in life. It is written, "But if thou shalt indeed obey his voice, and do all that I speak; then I will be an enemy unto thine enemies, and an adversary unto thine adversaries." (Exodus 23:22).It is written, "Let them be as chaff before the wind: and let the angel of the Lord chase them. Let their way be dark and slippery: and let the angel of the Lord persecute them." Psalms 35:5-6

~The Angels of God are agents of deliverance

Every time you find yourself in any kind of imprisonment, you must pray and ask the angels of God to intervene. It is written, "And, behold, the angel of the Lord came upon him, and a light shined in the prison: and he smote Peter on the side, and raised him up, saying, Arise up quickly. And his chains fell off from his hands. And the angel said unto him, Gird thyself, and bind on thy sandals. And so he did. And he saith unto him, Cast thy garment about thee, and follow me." Acts 12:7-8

Prayer:

Lord God, I pray you would help me to be sensitive to your Spirit in every situation. Help me know when I'm being directed by you and give me the faith to obey the leading of the Holy Spirit. In Jesus name, Amen!

CONCLUSION

"The angel of the Lord encampeth round about them that fear him, and delivereth them."
Psalms 34:7

The truth is God's angels are all over you. It is time to seek the face of the Lord in prayers and in thanksgiving. May this book help you activate angelic re-enforcement in your in the mighty Name of Jesus.

"Therefore if any man be in Christ, he is a new creature: old things are passed away; behold, all things are become new. Now repeat this Prayer after me." 2 Cor 5:17

What must I do to determine my divine visitation?

To determine divine visitation you must be born again! The word says as many as received him, to them gave He power to become the sons of God. Even to them that believe on his name.

To qualify for divine visitation, do the following with sincerity—

1) Acknowledge that you are a sinner and that He died for you. (Romans 3:23)

2) Repent of your sins. (Acts 3:19, Luke 13:5, 2 Peter 3:9)

3) Believe in your heart that Jesus died for your sin. (Romans 10:10)

4) Confess Jesus as the Lord over your life. (Romans 10:10, Acts 2:21)

Now repeat this Prayer after me

Say Lord Jesus, I accept you today, as my Lord and my savior, forgive me of my sins wash me with your blood. Right now, I believe, I am sanctified, I am save, I am free, I am free from the Power of sin to serve the Lord Jesus. Thank you Lord for saving me. Amen.

Chapter 2   The Function of Angels

Congratulations: You are now...

A BORN AGAIN CHRISTIAN.
Again I say to you—

CONGRATULATIONS!

I will encourage you to join a bible believing church or join us on our weekly and Sunday worship services at 343 Sanford Avenue, Newark, New Jersey, 07106.

WISDOM KEYS

— Every Productive Society is a society heading to the top.

— Millions of Nigerians run away from Nigeria, very few Nigerians stay in Nigeria.

— My decision to return Nigeria is the will of God for my life.

— My short coming in America after 18 years, trained me to be wise, to think, reflect and reason appropriately.

— If you train your mind to reason it will train your hands to earn money.

— It is absurd to use the money of the heathen to build the kingdom of the living God.

— Every Ministry reveals its agenda and goal either at the beginning or at the end. Be careful of your life it is your first Ministry.

— The average American mind is conditioned for a continual quest to get new things and (discard the former) and throw away old things.

— When I considered well, my BMW jeep became my initial deposit for the work of the ministry in Nigeria.

— Money will never fall from any tree.

— Everyone is waiting for you to change your mind until you change your thinking nothing changes around you.

— Multiple academic degrees in other discipline gave me the chance to think, reflect and reason.

— What so everyone are thinking and reflecting at the moment reveals you to the time and the now factor .

— All events and intents are the product of precise thought processes, accurate reason every event is designed for a designated timeline.

— Wisdom is your ability to think, to create and invent. If you can think wise enough you will come out of penury.

— The distance between you and success is your creative ability to think reason and reflect accurate.

— Success is the result of hard work, commitment resolve and determination learning from past mistakes and failing.

— If you organize your mind you have organized your life and destiny.

— There is a thin line between success and failure. If you look above and beyond you are on your way to success.

— Wealth is your ability to think, power is your ability to reason and success is your ability to be informed.

— If you can make use of your mind by thinking and reasoning God will make use of your life and destiny.

— Think and Be Great.

— Reflect, Reason, Think and Be Great.

— Famous people are born of woman.

— That you will make it is your intention; that you will survive is your resolve, that you will succeed with changes is your determination, personal efforts and hard work.

— No man was born a failure. Lack of vision is the end product of failure.

— Working with mental patients encourages and aspire me to be a productive observant and dedicated to my assignment.

— Successful people are not magicians, it is the will power combined with hard work, and determination and a resolve to succeed that make them succeed.

— In the unequivocal state of the mind, intention is not a location or a position it is the state of the mind.

— So many people think, that they think. The mind is used to think, reflect, and reason. You will remain blind with your eye open until you can see with your mind by thinking.

— There is no favoritism in accurate and precise calculation.

— Although knowledge is power, information is the key and gateway to a great future.

— It will take the hand of God to move the hand of man.

— With the backing of the great wise God, nothing will disconnect you from your inheritance.

— As long as you have wisdom and understanding of God, Satan and evil cannot manipulate your life and destiny.

— You have come this far by yourself judgment and decision you have made in the past, now lean and listen to God for another dimension of greatness.

— Great people are common people it is extra ordinary effort and the price of sacrifice that produces greatness.

— As a mental direct care worker I saw a great pastor and a motivational speaker within myself.

— Menial job does not reduce your self-worth, until you resolve to achieve greatness see greatness in all you do; you will never count in your community.

— The principle of Jesus will solve your gambling and addiction problems.

— The man of Jesus will lead you into heaven.

— Everyone have their self-appraisal and what they think about you. Until you discover yourself other opinion about you will alter the real you.

— Supervisors and directors are just a position in the chain of command in a work place. Never allow your supervisor hierarchy to alter your opinion about yourself.

— Everyone can come out of debt if they make up their mind.

— That I am not a decision maker at work does not diminish my contribution to my world.

— Although it appears like it was a poor decision to accept a direct care employment at a psychiatric hospital as I reflect of my nine years of experience, it became apparent that I have learnt and experienced enough for my next assignment in life.

— Self-encouragement and determination is a resolve of the heart.

— If you are determined to make a difference, and do the things that make a difference you will eventually make a difference.

— Good things do not come easy.

— Short cuts will cut your life short.

— Those who look ahead move ahead.

— Life is all about making an impact. In your life time strive to make an impact in your community.

— Make friends and connect with people who are moving ahead of you in life.

— If you can look around well you have come a long way in your life, made a lot of difference and realized a lot of success in life.

— If you are my old friend, hurry up to reach out to me before I become a stranger to you.

— Everything I am blessed with inspirations from God, that change my definition and interpretation of the world around me.

— I thought I was stagnant and lonely until I looked around and noticed my children running around and my wife cooking.

— At 40 I resigned my Job to seek the Lord forever.

— My ministry took a drastic rise to the top when the wisdom of God visited me with knowledge and understanding.

— You will be a better person, if you understand the characteristics of your personality – your mood swings, attitudes, and habits.

— It is the seed of love you sow into the heart of a child and a woman that you reap in due time.

— Love is not selfish, love share everything including the concealed secrets of the mind.

— As long as you have a prayer life and a bible; you will never feel lonely, rejected, and idle in the race of life.

— When good friends disconnect from you, let them go, they might have seen something new in a different direction.

— Confidence in yourself and in God is the only way to bring you out of captivity.

— Never train a child to waste his/her time.

— The mind is the greatest assets of a great future.

— You walk by common sense run by principles and fly by instruction.

— Those who fly in flight of life fly alone.

— Up in the air you are alone. No one can toll you accept the compass of knowledge and information.

— I have seen a towing vehicle I have seen a towing ship I have never seen a tolling airplane.

— I exercise my judgment and make a decision every minute of the day.

— Decisions are crucial, critical and vital with reference to your future.

— So many people wish for a great future. You can only work towards a great future.

— Your celebrity status began when you discovered your talent. What are you good at? Work at it with all commitment.

— Prayers will sustain you but the wisdom of God will prosper you.

— When I met Oyedepo, his teachings changed my perspective. But when I met Ibiyeomie; His teaching changed my perception.

— I will be successful in ministry if only I concentrate and focus my energy in the work of the ministry.

Chapter 2   The Function of Angels

— It took the late Dr. Vincent Pearle Norman's book to open my mind towards kingdom success.

CHAPTER 3

PRAYER OF SALVATION

"Neither is there salvation in any other: for there is none other name under heaven given among men, whereby we must be saved."
Acts 4:12

Salvation, simply means deliverance of our soul from sin and the destruction of the devil. If we must make it with God in eternity, we must genuinely recognize what we need to do in righteousness to live a new life with Jesus Christ.

What must I do to determine my divine visitation?

To determine divine visitation you must be born again! The word says as many as received him, to them gave He power to become the sons of God. Even to them that believe on his name.

To qualify for divine visitation, do the following with sincerity—

1) Acknowledge that you are a sinner and that He died for you. (Romans 3:23)

Chapter 3   Prayer of Salvation

2) Repent of your sins. (Acts 3:19, Luke 13:5, 2 Peter 3:9)

3) Believe in your heart that Jesus died for your sin. (Romans 10:10)

4) Confess Jesus as the Lord over your life. (Romans 10:10, Acts 2:21)

Now repeat this Prayer after me

Say Lord Jesus, I accept you today, as my Lord and my savior, forgive me of my sins wash me with your blood. Right now, I believe, I am sanctified, I am save, I am free, I am free from the Power of sin to serve the Lord Jesus. Thank you Lord for saving me. Amen.

Congratulations: You are now...

A BORN AGAIN CHRISTIAN.
Again I say to you—

CONGRATULATIONS!

I adjure you to watch the Spirit of God bear witness with your Spirit confirming His word with signs following. The word says The Spirit itself beareth witness with our spirit, that we are the children of God.

MIRACLE CARE OUTREACH

*"...But that the members should have
the same care one for another"*
1 Corinthians 12:25

We are all members of the body of Christ. Jesus commanded us to love our neighbor as ourselves. This includes caring for one another as a member of one body. True love is expressed in caring and giving. The word says for God so Love He gave….

Reach out to someone in need of Jesus, help someone in crisis find Christ. Look out and prove your love to Jesus by caring and inviting your friends and associates to find Jesus the Healer.

Invite your friends to our Home Care Cell Fellowship (Miracle chapel Intl Satellite fellowship) In the USA at 33 Schley Street, Newark, New Jersey, 07112. Home Care Cell fellowship Group meets every Tuesday at 6:00pm-7:00pm.

If you are in Nigeria—**MIRACLE OF GOD MINISTRIES**, aka **"MIRACLE CHAPEL INTL"** Mpama –Egbu-Owerri Imo state Nigeria.

LIFE IS NOT ALL ABOUT DURATION— BUT ITS ALL ABOUT DONATION

What does the above statement mean?....

Life consists not in the accumulation of material wealth. (Luke 12:15) But it's all about liberality...meaning - what you can give and share with others. Proverb11:25. When you live for others—You live forever - because you out live your generation by the legacy you live behind after you depart into glory to be with the Lord. But when you live to yourself - you are reduced to self—you are easily forgotten when you die and depart in glory. Permit me to admonish you today to live your life to be a blessing to a soul connected to you today. I want you to know that so many souls are connected and looking up to you, and through you so many souls will be saved and rescued from destruction. Will you disciple someone today to find Jesus Christ?

As a genuine Christian; it is your duty to evangelize Jesus Christ to all you meet on your way. Jesus is still in the healing business-Jesus is still doing miracles from time of old to now. Therefore tell someone about Jesus Christ today, disciple and bring them to Church. (John 1:45) Philip findeth Nathanael....

Please to prove the sincerity of your love for God today; please become a soul winner. The dignity of your Christianity is hidden in your boldness to proclaim and evangelize Jesus Christ to all you meet on your way. There is a question mark on the integrity of your Christianity until you become a life soul winner. Invite someone to join us worship the Lord Jesus this coming Sunday. Amen.

MIRACLE OF GOD MINISTRIES

PILLARS OF THE COMMISSION

We Believe Preach and Practice the following:

1) We believe and preach Salvation to every living human being

2) We believe and preach Repentance and forgiveness of sins

3) We believe and preach the baptism of the Holy Spirit and Spiritual gifts

4) We believe and teach the Prosperity

5) We believe and preach Divine Healing and Miracles (Signs & Wonder)

6) We believe and preach Faith

7) We believe and proclaim the Power of God (Supernatural)

8) We believe and proclaim Praise & Worship to God

9) We believe and preach Wisdom

10) We believe and preach Holiness (Consecration)

11) We believe and preach Vision

12) We believe and teach the Word of God

13) We believe and teach Success

14) We believe and practice Prayer

15) We believe and teach Deliverance

These 15 stones form the Pillars of Our Commission. Become part of this church family and follow this great move of God.

MY HEART FELT PRAYER FOR YOU

It is not only my desire, but my uttermost vision that you encounter the Lord Jesus Christ as your personal Lord and savior. You must be born again. As ruthless as it may sound today, it is my ministry to see you saved and engrafted into the kingdom of God. Most of us do not really understand what it means to be "saved." The word "Salvation", literally means deliverance of our soul and spirit from the destruction of the devil. But until we repent, we cannot be saved. Every one of us must genuinely make plans to make heaven at last. "For what shall it profit a man if he gains the whole world but loses his soul?"

Now let me pray for you:

Holy Spirit of God, we give you thanks and praise. Lord I pray that the eyes of our understanding may be opened today. May we put faith to work by taking action in our lives, in the mighty Name of Jesus. Amen.

PUT YOUR ANGELS TO WORK

You are in the best position to put your angels to work. No man can help you do this in your life. It is written "Beware of him, and obey his voice, provoke him not; for he will not pardon your transgressions: for my name is in him. But if thou shalt indeed obey his voice, and do all that I speak; then I will be an enemy unto thine enemies, and an adversary unto thine adversaries." Exodus 23:21-22

CHAPTER 4
ABOUT THE AUTHOR

Rev Franklin N Abazie is the founding and Presiding Pastor of Miracle of God Ministries with headquarters in Newark, New Jersey USA and a branch church in Owerri- Imo State Nigeria. He is following the footsteps of one of his mentors, Oral Roberts (Healing Evangelist) of the blessed memory. The Lord passed Oral Roberts healing mantle two days before he went to be with the Lord at age 91 into the hand of healing evangelist-Rev Franklin N Abazie in a vision.

In all his services the Power and Presence of God is present to heal all in his audience. He is an ordained man of God with a Healing Ministry reviving the healing and miracle ministry of Jesus Christ of Nazareth.

Pastor Franklin N Abazie, is called by God with a unique mandate: **"THE MOMENT IS DUE TO IMPACT YOUR WORLD THROUGH THE REVIVAL OF THE HEALING & MIRACLE MINISTRY OF JESUS CHRIST OF NAZARETH**

"I AM SENDING YOU TO RESTORE HEALTH UNTO THEE AND I WILL HEAL

THEE OF THY WOUNDS. SAID THE LORD OF HOST"

Rev. Abazie is a gifted ardent Teacher of the word of God who operates also in the office of a Prophet, generating and attracting undeniable signs & wonders, special miracles and healings, with apostolic fireworks of the Holy Ghost. He is the founding and presiding senior Pastor of this fast growing Healing ministry. He has written over 86 inspirational, healing and transforming books covering almost all aspect of divine healing and life. He is happily married and blessed with children.

BOOKS BY REV FRANKLIN N ABAZIE

1) Commanding Abundance
2) The outcome of faith
3) Understanding the secret of prevailing prayers.
4) Understanding the secret of the man God uses
5) Activating my due Season
6) Overcoming Divine Verdicts
7) The Outcome of Divine Wisdom
8) Understanding God's Restoration Mandate
9) Walking in the Victory and Authority of the truth
10) Gods Covenant Exemption
11) Destiny Restoration Pillars
12) Provoking Acceptable Praise
13) Understanding Divine Judgment
14) Activating Angelic Re-enforcement
15) Provoking Un-Merited Favor
16) The Benefits of the Speaking Faith
17) Understanding Divine Arrangement
18) Understanding Divine Healing
19) The Mystery of Endurance
20) Obeying Divine Instructions
21) Understanding the Voice of God
22) Never give up on Hope
23) The prevailing Power of faith
24) Understanding Divine Prosperity
25) The Reward of Prayer
26) Covenant Keys to Answered Prayers
27) Activating the Forces of Vengeance
28) Put your faith to work

29) Where is your trust?
30) The Audacity of the Blood of Jesus
31) Redeeming Your Days
32) The Foce of Vision
33) Breaking the shackles of Family curses
34) Wisdom for Marriage Stability
35) The winners Faith
36) The Prayer solution
39) The power of Prayer
40) Prayer strategy
41) The prayer that works
42) Walking in Forgiveness
43) The power of the grace of God
44) The power of Persistence
45) Overcoming Divine verdicts
46) The audacity of the blood of Jesus.
47) The prevailing power of the blood of Jesus
49) The benefit of the speaking faith.
50) Fearless faith
51) Redeeming Your Days.
52) The Supernatural Power of Prophecy
53) The companionship of the Holy Spirit
54) Understanding Divine Judgement
55) Understanding Divine Prosperity
56) Dominating Controlling Forces
57) The winners Faith
58) Destiny Restoration Pillars
59) Developing Spiritual Muscles
60) Inexplicable faith
61) The lifestyle of Prayer

62) Developing a positive attitude in life.
63) The mystery of Divine supply
64) Encounter with God's Power
65) Walking in love
66) Praying in the Spirit
67) How to provoke your testimony
68) Walking in the reality of the anointing
69) The reality of new birth
70) The price of freedom
71 The Supernatural power of faith
72 The Power of Persistence
73) The intellectual components of Redemption.
74) Overcoming Fear
75) The Force of Vision
76) Overcoming Prevailing Challenges
77) The Power of the Grace of God
78) My life & Ministry
79) The Mystery of Praise

MIRACLE OF GOD MINISTRIES

*NIGERIA CRUSADE
2012*

MIRACLE OF GOD MINISTRIES

NIGERIA CRUSADE 2012

MIRACLE OF GOD MINISTRIES

*NIGERIA CRUSADE
2012*

www.ingramcontent.com/pod-product-compliance
Lightning Source LLC
Chambersburg PA
CBHW020624300426
44113CB00007B/776